# Naked Rib

*poems by*

# Deborrah Corr

*Finishing Line Press*
Georgetown, Kentucky

# Naked Rib

## ACKNOWLEDGMENTS

I gratefully acknowledge the editors of the following journals where these
poems first appeared:

*Amethyst Review*: "I Was Eve"
*Catamaran*: "Bywater Bay"
*Crosswinds Poetry Journal*: "Girl in the Barn With Paper and a Pencil," "It
Shouldn't Have Been a Mobile Phone"
*Grand Little Things*: "Death of a Carpenter," "In Old Growth"
*Literary Mama*: "Goat in the Corner"
*The McNeese Review*: "Daughter in Blue"
*The Main Street Rag:* "Back to Daddy's Living Room"
*New Feathers Anthology*: "Forgetting the Shape of Home"
*Raven Chronicles Journal*: "Eating the Earth"
*Sequoia Speaks*: "Learning the Language of Hunger," "Bird at My Door"
*Streetlight Magazine*: "The Owl"
*Sunlight Press*: "His Name Came Back to Me Today"
*Thimble Magazine*: "Planting Heather at the New House"

Publisher: Leah Huete de Maines
Editor: Christen Kincaid
Cover Art: William Corr
Author Photo: Kent Bush
Cover Design: Elizabeth Maines McCleavy


Order online: www.finishinglinepress.com
also available on amazon.com

Author inquiries and mail orders:
Finishing Line Press
PO Box 1626
Georgetown, Kentucky 40324
USA

# Contents

*In Memory of*
*Peter and Amanda*

*For*
*Kent, Will and Joy*
*who keep me living*

# I Was Eve

that naked rib, weaving through tiny words
on the tissue pages of my bible.
I lifted her out of the ink and drank her.

The curves of her body glowed,
clothed in the warmth of a young sun
that seeped through the leaves of Eden.

Eden, that scrim of perfection,
paper thin and easily torn.

She had seen the serpent, long and supple,
wound around branches and coiled
at the base of trees. It glided a path

in the soil and grass. Unrestricted.
How would it feel, its one cord-like
muscle massaging its way all over

her body. She wanted to dance with it
twined around her torso. Oh, the tingle
of its tongue on her skin.

Temptation to know, to taste.
I shake the lock on the garden gate.

## Eating the Earth

I did it with a spoon I stole
quietly from the kitchen,
away from my mother's eyes,
an urgent endeavor.

There was a special spot
out back behind the house
where the dirt was soft,
a powdery dust.

It coated the roof of my mouth,
got gritty on my teeth,
mixed with the wet of my tongue
and crusted on my lips.

Deep satisfaction,
I remember it still:
ingesting the body
of the beloved—
my first communion.

## Girl In the Barn with Paper and a Pencil

I wanted the pencil to curve a calf. I wanted
my eyes to pull my hand along the rise
of flank, along the bumpy road of back,
up the hill of neck and render his tender face
on the flat surface of the page.
      Flat?
             No.
I wanted his electric hum
to run my body, my hands to spill him
on the small pale square. I wanted
the prickles of hay poking my skin
to needle me alive like this creature
pushed into the world as bewildered as I
who wanted to be new like this calf.
I wanted everything new to be etched,
to be chiseled into stone, into boulders
clogging and diverting all straight roads.
I wanted not to be locked in a line
of wooden desks, the apples of crayon red
pinned and curled in the yellowing orchard
of a wall. I wanted the pencil tip to pierce
the white plane of page, to carve open ribs,
free beating hearts, break down
all the fences on the farm before this baby
grew to be meat on the table. I wanted
to know I could draw, I could pull down
the whole world into a few gray lines
of newborn calf still sticky
with its mother's blood.

## Just Another Fruit

Sun on dew-wet leaves. I'm dressed
in autumn and apple tree ready.

Ready to climb where globes are reddened
and ripe for molars to ache in the crunch.

Long reach for a branch, and never mind
the scrape of bark. My finger blots the blood.

I bring it to my mouth and love the metallic
taste of me. Through the window I see

my brother blankly staring at TV.
The first apple hangs in temptation.

A crash of glass as my imagination
throws this ball and hits my brother. But

I am not here for that kind of pleasure.
I sink my teeth into it instead. A crunch.

Saliva's rush fills my canyon mouth,
wets my lips, dribbles on my shirt.

Sweet, tart gravenstein. Its flesh
dissolving. Peel catching between my teeth

for my tongue to worry later. Up and outward
I inch, risking a fall that might break

a bone again. My mother's voice weaves
through my limbs like a wind. I hang,

just another fruit, ripened, ready,
waiting to be picked.

## Mother of Twelve
*—for Lily Faye, my mother*

Here comes that youngest of mine
                        bawling again, all snot and tears.
                        I'm plain worn out with her.
Blood spots like freckles on her arm,
                        a wrecked rose in her hand.
                                  (Pick them, child, and they
                                      pick you back.)
Girl, you will bleed
                  and bleed and bleed again.
            You came in on a flood of my blood
              and, female, the earth will pull it down
              from between your legs
                    like you were the tide itself.
           In the craving of scarlet moments your womb
              gets filled, stuffed with one baby after another
                    'til you are drained pale.

I know she wants a path that's painted with petals. I did.
           Wanted them sprinkled all over my covers.
                  But it's a bed of thorns that slash, that puncture
                  every bloated hope you had.
 You can drown in all that red—
           trying to staunch the wounds on a gunshot boy,
              the dog bleeding out on the side of the road,
                  the headless chicken you chopped
                  because you need to feed a family.

Now her head's in my lap,
           cheeks petal smooth,
           eyes big as full blossoms.
She asks for that story again,
           the one with the princess, the rose,
           the thorn, the prince.

I'll tell her a different tale—
        a forest of brambles that prick you all over.
        The magic is in how it thickens your skin.

I'll tell her, but she's drifting off to sleep,
the blue veins pulsing in her tiny wrists.

## Back to Daddy's Living Room

Maybe I slam the door. Get him
to turn around and scowl at me.
Get him for a moment to raise his head
from that eternal game of solitaire
there at his table in the corner
with its bare light bulb, its string
dangling like a thought he forgot.
Maybe I pull on that string. Get him
to stop the *slap, slap* of cards
on the scarred wooden surface, a ragged
percussion downing the howls, the squabbles,
the kids. Maybe I approach, as ever,
with the weather gone dry in my mouth,
my stomach's tightness lashed to its rail.
Maybe I stand right behind the memorized
back of him, the overall's blue straps rising
like narrow paths over his shoulders. Maybe
my fingers, so accustomed to the shape of grudge,
trace those roads across his back and feel
the throb of flightless birds caged under his ribs.

## The Owl

Half concealed on the branch in new oak leaves,
silent, the barred owl watches with giant eyes,
Its body, all of a piece, no indentation
even for a neck. If I could reach high enough,
my fingers might stroke it in one long move
from head to base, flat-handed, barely a touch,
the slightest tickle of feather, like the way,
as a child, I'd kneel by muddy puddles, hover
my hand over brown water, lower my arm
bit by slow bit, trying to touch the surface
without a ripple, no disturbance. Like how
I'd learned to stand so still I could study snakes,
my eyes fixed on the thin wire of their bodies,
no noise to make them curve an S into the brush.
Like how I'd slink away from a room of yelling voices
before a hand could aim a slap at the side of my head.
Adept at the sidestep, but swallowing a fill of shame
as I left. Adept at silent watching from a branch,
my feathers still, as if formed by a potter,
molded and fired to hard immobility.
Only careful hands prevent the shattering.
I don't want to shatter any fragile thing,
any small thing that glitters in the light,
dazzling for its moment. I don't want to be
the shattered one, a vase left close to the edge.
My talons clutch the branch so hard it could bleed.
Unlike this owl who sees the wriggling in the grass,
and with a sudden swoop, fueled by fiery desire,
dives into fear, and, with mouth and feet
extracts exactly what it needs, blood and all.

## Dangerous Swerves

Twelve years old, striding on
a small town's broken sidewalk,
she feels the rub of skin
inside soft pedal pushers.

She slides her palms down her sides,
cups the curves she finds,
the swell of hips so new
she wonders who

wears her body now.
Some fleshy girl, who swerves
and surges with power,
and mingles with the boys

who smoke behind the bleachers.
Her lips turn up at the corners
when she feels that little lick
of danger.

## His Name Came Back to Me Today

unfolding itself from the creases
of memory. For months, years
I couldn't conjure up its syllables.
I can't remember the contours of his face
nor how his hair rested on his scalp.
I only recall the shape of him
hovered over me in the bed
I'd travelled across states
to crawl into. As if I needed
the outlines of a new skin
after I'd shrugged off my own
too quickly, trusting that the moment
loved me, that I could step out
into nothing and be held up
by friendly prevailing winds.
Everything I owned in two canvas bags.
So young, so full of heat, not yet
tumbled down the hillside of magic.
Those winds muffled the hoof beats
of humiliation racing the Trailways,
shucking beads of sweat
until they overtook me. Four days,
thirty dollars in my pocket,
and I was back on the bus. Back
to where I thought I'd closed
a door forever and found
my dried-up skin laid out
and waiting on the floor,
the letters of his name
dismembered among my things.

# Learning the Language of Hunger

Those mewling cries dug inside your dream
of cats yowling in the yard. The light
lifted the lids sealing your sleep.

At last, the sound grew fingers
that pulled you by the ears, shook you
to remember (How could you forget?)

this baby where you'd laid her for a nap
you took as yours. Motherhood so new
the call of hunger wafted out the window.

Your womb had opened like a reluctant
gate, pushing through a new life and you
to an earth of unfamiliar tongue.

Your breasts dripped a liquid not yet milk
enough. But how she latched on. Her suck
was strong, like she believed in you.

Your arms dull with slumber, you wondered
how you could learn this waking up,
how you would learn to be enough.

## Home Shore

Carried on the tsunami of a contracting uterus,
my son's eyes opened to a landscape of shape
and shadow. In silence he scanned the room.
Almost nothing moved but his tiny orbs.

And we, stunned again by miracle, watched as if
a raw god had emerged from a stone split
by lightning, a god with the power to unveil
a truth we'd sought since our own birth.

His eyes washed over our humble group,
an unfocused sweep, until our daughter
broke the hush with her high-pitched delight.
The wandering gaze stopped, landed soft

on the planes of her cheeks. And stayed there,
safe on this small shore. The home he knew.
This voice, the song he'd heard calling him
from across the ocean.

## Demeter

Why didn't I see it
when she was little?
Always picking flowers,
her fists full of stems.
Her face washed in wonder.
I didn't heed the warning.
I let her wander in the fields.
Now she's far afield.

She slammed the door,
disappeared down the street,
her hair streaming like ropes
that yanked my angry, guilty heart.

No help from Olympus or 9-1-1.
Alone, I scour I-Hop and Denny's,
the midnight haunts of runaways
and try to pry her whereabouts
from doped-up girls in halter tops
shivering on the Ave.

I've torn my hair, my clothes
in the school counselor's office
while the mothers in the hallways
nod at each other like they
could see this coming.

Oh, smug bitches, I scream
inside my car. If I could, I would
flatten this earth. Barren.
Scorch the harvests.   Nothing
on your shelves.   No water
from your spigots.   No flowers
in your manicured yards.

I should have known.
I do know Hades,
that dog of a brother,
panting lust, sniffing at me,
pawing at my chest
as soon as I grew breasts.

I should have seen him lurking,
dank in his dark underground,
beneath a field of daffodils.

I should have been watching.
I was careless, full of belief
that what I birthed
onto this earth
was mine to keep.

## Goat in the Corner

I snapped that moment, my vision
extended through the camera lens,
my finger on the shutter, opening
the diaphragm for the light needed
to capture them.

He's on one knee, his arms around
a baby goat. Its white legs dangle,
its ears flatten back. Our little daughter
leans her weight into his side, her hand
on the back of the kid's neck.
Her whole body sings with delight.

My past is printed on glossy paper. Flat,
with only memory to inflate it. I reach in
and feel the rub of her corduroy pants,
the slippery nylon puff on his down vest,
how his mustache tickled my cheek.
Her soft braids. The tug of the purple sweater
when I pulled it over her hair.

The head of the mother goat enters
the lower right corner. White, almost
faded now, frozen as she moved
to free her baby. Stopped in the act

that goat and I, rendered impotent.
Cancer, the camera, its shutter snapping
closed, first on him, then on her.
They're pinned inside this frame.
And we are fixed forever
staring in from the corner.

### Death of a Carpenter

It's raining nails as if the sky is cleaning shop.

It's raining my dead husband's hair as well,
the hair I shook from the pillow, clumps of it.

An unaccustomed clatter from the clouds,
cans of screws and bolts, old saws discarded.

Listen. Is there a sound as unfinished projects
fade? Can you hear a life lifting, just a hint

of music, a white vapor in its going.

## Opening the Storage Closet

It all falls out.
The shelves shout, "We've done enough."
They plunge themselves down the long
flight of stairs and let the front door slam.

It isn't time
for sorting, but there, on the floor, you find it—
his shirt, the one the color of winter sky,
cold in its lifelessness.

Shake it out.
The sleeves hang limp, no matter how much
breath your memory can blow.   You want.
You want.   You think you want his back
in the shirt, bending over to tie his shoes,
a thing he couldn't do at the end.

But this lemur,
its enormous eyes unblinking, is peeking
from beneath the collar. Its nail has snagged
a thread ready to unravel a true story
that you can't get your lips to tell.

## It Shouldn't Have Been a Mobile Phone

that rectangle connected to nothing
I could see. It should have had a cord
I could crawl down and shove the words
back along their course, a cord leading
to a Bakelite box with a dial I could rotate
backwards, make the call never come.
Or maybe the cell phone was perfect
for her message about cells, cells that got
the wrong message, that grew, surged,
swelled way out of their allotted space.
She once had an allotted place inside my body.
She was a life of rapidly growing cells,
her messages made of ripples and kicks
in a fluid that flooded her coming, an arrival
announced into a receiver we could wrap
our hands around and speak the news
we would never want to undo.

**His ghost in my morning shower**

assembles itself in the steam,
filmy, but taking all the space.
I stand there a wet beggar,

wanting what from this phantom?
He has no touch. He has no speech.
He lives in picture frames.

Eight years gone, his last breaths
choked out in a place we called
living room, not dying room.

Our daughter is dying,
lying just a room away,
her head denuded like his

cancer depleted
chemo defeated
she wants to go.

Has he come with fleshless fingers
to pull her next to the bones
of his nonexistent chest,

trying to remember
what a beating heart feels like?
He is made of mist. He fades.

I am alone. And he has taken
his expertise on dying
with him to the grave.

## Daughter in Blue

Those last days a shuttle dragged
the weft of me through the warp
of a tapestry I wanted to rip apart
with both hands.

I thought it was gold she wove
when she called me to lie beside her,
to hold her hand into the gap
between waking pain and sleep.

But I didn't expect the blue. A light
seeped under the blinds to find her,
to trace an azure line down the profile
of her forehead, nose and chin,

as if night had dipped its brush
in tenderness and stroked her face.
As if it spoke in a whisper:
*this, always.*

## Dear Devil's Ivy,

I should have known by your name
you would persist. Your one long
tendril reaches out of the jumble,
the jungle of your pot, climbs up
over the bricks of a dormant fireplace,
forms a fringe on top of its screen.

I should have known I'd feel guilty
each time I look in your direction,
the way I felt the itch of sin when in
my childhood, your namesake hung
over every pleasure. Your leaves
droop, tips pointing down, panting
for the drink I've thoughtlessly withheld.

You can't kill that one, my daughter said,
when she chose you at Ikea.
On top of the cabinet you grew,
spread in every direction, vines
trailing toward floor, reaching for walls,
as abundant as the waterfall of her hair,
until it couldn't outlast the chemo.
You and I survived on parched soil
as she withered away.

Then I trimmed you, so you'd fit
the packing box and promised
if you would withstand the move,
I'd take better care. I apologize.
It's a failing of mine not to notice
what thirsts around me, or in me.
Sometimes I tell myself it's all dry dust.
But there you are waving your limp
banners of survival, calling me to pay
attention to what I've been given.

## Planting Heather at the New House

A cube of soil so rich I want to eat
my mother's chocolate cake,
but this won't crumble. It holds its shape
when I perch it on my palm
after peeling away the black plastic.

Translucent roots like ghostly wire
are locked in a grip that won't let go,
despite my pressure to loosen, to take
the form of the hole I've made
in this new bed.

I'm wearing your sweater,
the green one that zips up the side,
the one that housed your warmth
in those last cold days. Its fibers,
infused with flakes of your skin,
settle around me, trying
to remake your shape.

## Maze of Grief

These hallways,
tall blank walls,
this is no place to hang
pictures that snag your skin
and make you bleed.

What led you here again?
A random thought,
a painful twist of the neck,
too many days sunless,
how the months run out
of time and start the count all over.

With these blinders
on each side of your eyes
there's nowhere
but back and forth,
dull feet tramping
the same plantless ground.

Your breath hides inside
the corset of your ribs,
rigid against what threat?
The thieves have already
ransacked your house.
They left the doors wide open.

## Bird at My Door

It's lying limp on the mat, victim of the glass door
that looks like escape when the hawk swoops by.
A mound that barely fills the cup of my hand.
A flutter alive under feathers, a shudder
of tiny beak as if a call would leak, a *dee-dee-dee*
of distress. And who would come? I lift it
to a nest of towels and rags. I lay my head
next to its black mask and watch the filmy lid
on a single beaded eye close and open.
It's no help to say I'm sorry. We own the door.
We own the feeder only feet away, and I
can't justify that position with my joy
of watching the zig-zag path they fly to swarm
the feeder, the sound of insistent kazoos if
they find it empty. All we wanted was to feed them,
not make them easy prey to hawk and door.
So I stay, attending to vibrations of body,
attempts to rise, then fall. Letting my own breath come
and leave. I've done this before—waiting while life
decides where it will go. How big is the life inside
this body, the size of a snack for a hawk? Surely
as big as the life in mine protected by doors
and walls. Night falls. Attention gives way to sleep.
Next morning it's gone. No way to tell if predator
or flight, no comfort from conclusion. Nor can
I pretend it's a gift, this small thing left,
this feather tiny as breath.

## In Old Growth

The planet and its forest pivot far enough
for the sun to stream between silent giants.

Light switches on. Bracken and cedar boughs
are serving plates of yellow gold.

Salal dazzles like tables of silver jewelry.
A heart has to fill with something like joy

or gratitude. The forest asks for nothing.
In its tall, rooted silence it withstands us.

Beneath the soil, its network will never
even speak of our passing.

## Forgetting the Shape of Home

I made a bed of soil
in my mother's garden,

earth molding to
the shape of my body,

I lifted fists full of dirt
and watched

as it filtered back
in a flow to the ground,

my eyes unfocused,
lost in sensation,

the sky benevolent
above the planet

with its own
heartbeat, the *lub-dub*

that rocks an infant
in its mother's womb.

When did that sound
grow faint in my ear?

When did I forget
how to shape my body

to fit the contours
of my home.

## Bywater Bay

Lucky there was a boat for crossing the bay,
a battered yellow rowboat you had to carry
down a rocky beach into freezing water
wishing the tide was high because you had
nine more trips back up to the car
and down that beach again with water jugs,
canvas clothing bags, banged-up cooler,
sleeping bags, and kids.

Lucky to find life jackets, two of them,
dirty and smelling of mold, to buckle on
the kids and perch them on the center plank.
One adult pushed off the boat, the other rowed,
aiming for the one smooth stretch of beach
on the other rocky shore, where a giant log
served as shelf for the tubs, jugs, bags, and kids
you carried up this beach.

Lucky winter storms hadn't washed away
the wooden steps that rose up the bank
and into woods and lucky the tree
fallen over the trail was easy to climb around.
Other fall-downs, covered in ferns and moss,
like walls, bordered the path to the cabin
with its sagging roof at the base of Douglas firs
so tall their tops were only visible with
an uncomfortable backward bend.

Lucky, in dripping wet, to get
a fire started in the pit, cook
oysters pried from rocks at low tide,
rocks that twisted your ankles
and made you wish you'd brought
the other shoes.

Lucky to remember those days,
glint of sun on wet leaves, pockets
heavy with collected stones, smell
of smoke in morning air, the four of you,
shoulders touching, pushing close
to fire's warmth, smoke lifting away
to be lost in the highest branches.

## With Thanks

My thanks to the many poets and friends who have accompanied me in the writing of these poems: my superb poetry revision partners—Wendy, Ariel, and Seth; the monthly Monday night group—Carla, Ginger, Peggy, Bob, and Alma; and the Women Writers Group—Arni, Sandy, Susan, Ariel, Casey, Kim, Karen, Amy. You mean so much to me.

My loving gratitude to my talented son, William Corr, who created the cover art for this book.

**Deborrah Corr** is a poet living in Seattle. She considers herself most fortunate to be able to devote her days to pursuing her love of poetry. She has worked with many teachers at Hugo House and online. Her work has appeared in the *McNeese Review, Catamaran Literary Reader, Sunlight Press,* and several others. This is her debut chapbook.

The twelfth child in a family of agricultural workers, Deborrah grew up in the Yamhill Valley of Oregon where she spent summers picking strawberries, pole beans, blackberries and many other crops. Her free time was spent roaming the woods and living inside her imagination. She remembers writing her first poem hiding behind a lilac bush in the front yard of her childhood home.

Higher education led her to a degree in drama from the University of Washington and later a master's degree in human development from Pacific Oaks College. Deborrah worked as a kindergarten teacher in Seattle Public Schools.

When not writing, the poet makes quilts, reads, gardens, and volunteers for the American Cancer Society. She lives happily with her supportive husband, Kent Bush. Dinner and game nights with her son, Will, and her daughter-in-law, Joy, are among her greatest delights.

www.deborrahcorr.com

www.ingramcontent.com/pod-product-compliance
Lightning Source LLC
Chambersburg PA
CBHW022052080426
42734CB00009B/1318